W9-COY-291

A GUIDE TO YOUR GOVERNMENT

Meet the HOUSE OF REPRESENTATIVES

By Therese Shea

Gareth Stevens
Publishing

Please visit our website, www.garethstevens.com. For a free color catalog of all our high-quality books, call toll free 1-800-542-2595 or fax 1-877-542-2596.

Library of Congress Cataloging-in-Publication Data

Shea, Therese.
Meet the House of Representatives / Therese Shea.
    p. cm. — (A guide to your government)
Includes index.
ISBN 978-1-4339-7253-9 (pbk.)
ISBN 978-1-4339-7254-6 (6-pack)
ISBN 978-1-4339-7252-2 (library binding)
1. United States. Congress. House—Juvenile literature. 2. Legislators—United States—Juvenile literature. I. Title.
JK1319.S52 2012
328.73′072—dc23

2012005939

First Edition

Published in 2013 by
Gareth Stevens Publishing
111 East 14th Street, Suite 349
New York, NY 10003

Copyright © 2013 Gareth Stevens Publishing

Designer: Daniel Hosek
Editor: Kristin Rajczak

Photo credits: Cover, pp. 1, 19 Alex Wong/Getty Images; p. 5 SuperStock/Getty Images; p. 7 (White House) Lambert/Getty Images; p. 7 (Supreme Court) Steve Heap/Shutterstock.com; p. 7 (Capitol) Lissandra/Shutterstock.com; p. 9 MaxFX/Shutterstock.com; p. 11 NationalAtlas.gov; p. 12 Scott Olson/Getty Images; p. 13 Ryan Kelly/Congressional Quarterly/Getty Images; p. 15 (main image) Tim Sloan/AFP/Getty Images; p. 15 (Nixon) Keystone/Hulton Archive/Getty Images; p. 16 Chip Somodevilla/Getty Images; pp. 17, 21 Mark Wilson/Getty Images; p. 23 Tom Williams/Roll Call/Getty Images; p. 25 (all images) Bloomberg/Getty Images; p. 27 Bill Clark/Roll Call/Getty Images.

Printed in the United States of America

CPSIA compliance information: Batch #CS12GS: For further information contact Gareth Stevens, New York, New York at 1-800-542-2595.

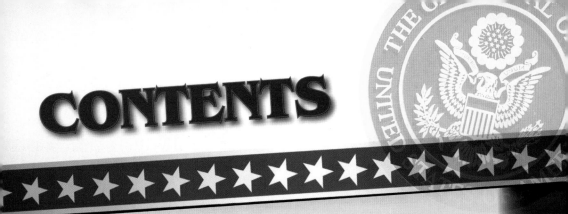

CONTENTS

Words in the glossary appear in **bold** type
the first time they are used in the text.

BEGINNING AGAIN

After the American Revolution, the Founding Fathers of the United States faced a challenge: How could they create a government that would truly represent the will of its citizens? They didn't want a king or other kind of ruler who could misuse power. The first plan for a US government was outlined in the Articles of Confederation. After several years, however, this **constitution** proved to be too weak. So much control lay with the states that the central, or federal, government couldn't raise taxes or organize a national army.

The country's leaders met again in 1787 and worked on a new constitution. This document, our US Constitution, balanced power between the federal and state governments. It created a government that divided responsibilities among three branches and provided "checks" for each branch's powers.

FEDERAL *Fact*

Among the representatives at the Constitutional Convention were George Washington, Benjamin Franklin, and Alexander Hamilton.

The Constitutional Convention

Fifty-five state representatives met in Philadelphia, Pennsylvania, in 1787. For about 4 months, they tried to fix the weaknesses of the Articles of Confederation. It wasn't an easy task. James Madison, the man behind replacing the Articles with a new Constitution, thought a stronger federal government could strengthen the nation. However, a group called Anti-Federalists opposed a stronger central government, fearing states would lose their power. Madison suggested a three-branch government to support both states' rights and federal strength.

The members of the Constitutional Convention signed the Constitution on September 17, 1787, in Philadelphia, Pennsylvania. The Constitution then went to the states to be officially approved, or ratified, by them.

The new US government kicked into action in 1789. The federal government was made up of the legislative branch, the executive branch, and the judicial branch.

The legislative branch, Congress, is the lawmaking arm of the government. It's made up of two parts, or houses: the Senate and the House of Representatives. The president heads the executive branch. It's his job to enforce the laws created by the legislative branch. He also has the power to reject, or veto, a legislative bill, which is a written proposal for a new law. The judicial branch is the federal court system headed by the highest court, the US Supreme Court. The Supreme Court hears cases dealing with the laws of the nation to make sure the laws agree with the Constitution. The federal courts have even more duties, including trying criminals charged with breaking federal laws.

FEDERAL Fact

Just as the president can "check" the power of Congress by vetoing a bill, Congress can "check" the president by overriding his veto or **impeaching** him if he commits a crime.

John Quincy Adams

John Quincy Adams was the only ex-president to become a member of the House. He was elected in 1830, after losing the race for reelection to the White House just 2 years before. He became famous for taking on the House's "gag rule," which kept citizens' antislavery **petitions** from being considered. Adams led the opposition to end the "gag rule." While in the House in 1848, Adams had a stroke and died just days later.

All legislative activities in the US House of Representatives begin and end in the House Chamber in the Capitol Building in Washington, DC.

7

WHY TWO HOUSES?

Why are there are two houses of Congress? At the Constitutional Convention, each state's representatives worried about how much power states would have over federal laws. States with many people, such as Virginia, thought they should have more representation. States with fewer people, such as Georgia, thought all states should have an equal say. The compromise was a bicameral, or two-house, Congress: the Senate and the House of Representatives.

Each state has an equal number of senators—two—bringing the total number in the US Senate today to 100. Each state's number of representatives is based on its population. The more people in the state, the more representatives it has. As of 2011, the House had 435 voting representatives. This number has been fixed since 1913, though the nation's population has risen.

Number of State Representatives in 1789

Massachusetts
8

New Hampshire
6

New York
6

Connecticut
5

Pennsylvania
8

Rhode Island
1

New Jersey
4

Delaware
1

Virginia
10

Maryland
6

North Carolina
5

South Carolina
5

Georgia
3

No matter how small the population of a state, it's promised at least one representative in the House.

The Three-Fifths Compromise

A question arose: How would slaves be counted in a state's population? Those opposed to slavery wished only to count free persons. This meant a state whose population included slaves would have fewer representatives than a similar state whose population contained all free persons. Both free and slave states needed to ratify the Constitution if it was to become law. A compromise was reached. A slave would be counted as three-fifths of a person.

THE PEOPLE'S HOUSE

The first House of Representatives had 65 members, one for every 30,000 Americans. After the first national **census**, the number grew to 106. Currently, each of the 435 members of the House represents about 600,000 people.

The House is often called the "people's house" of Congress. The members of the House have always been chosen directly by citizens. Representatives serve an area of their state called a congressional district and are elected by voters in that district.

The number of representatives in the House hasn't changed in many years. However, it's **reapportioned** every 10 years according to the census. This means state legislatures redraw the lines of the congressional districts to match population changes. The number of representatives a state has may change at this time, too.

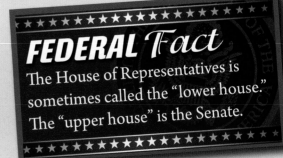

FEDERAL *Fact*
The House of Representatives is sometimes called the "lower house." The "upper house" is the Senate.

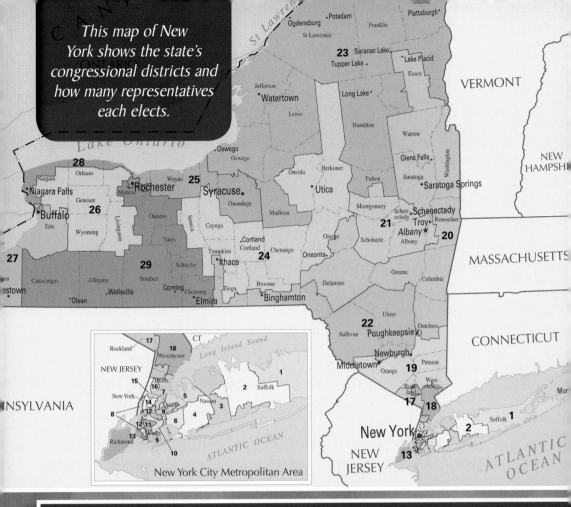

This map of New York shows the state's congressional districts and how many representatives each elects.

New York City Metropolitan Area

Gerrymandering

In 1812, the Massachusetts state legislature arranged congressional district lines to give an advantage to Republicans in elections. Governor Elbridge Gerry approved the arrangement. A newspaper editor thought one district looked like a salamander and made up the term "gerrymander." Today, arranging new congressional districts to give a political party an advantage is called "gerrymandering." This practice is illegal as redistricting occurs to reflect population changes, not to give any party an unfair advantage.

11

To be elected a member of the House of Representatives, a person must be at least 25 years old. A representative must have been a US citizen for at least 7 years and live in the state that they wish to represent. Though members serve a 2-year term, there is no limit on the number of times they can be reelected.

Because representatives spend just 2 years in office, they're more likely to act according to their **constituents**' wishes. If they don't, they won't win reelection. On the other hand, the Founding Fathers may have allowed senators a 6-year term in office so that they wouldn't vote only according to the current popular opinion. Hopefully, they'd vote according to the long-term effects of a law or decision.

Representative Jesse Jackson Jr. meets a group of constituents.

Representatives often invite the media to hear them give speeches and press conferences. This helps them keep their constituents informed.

Other Representatives

As of 2011, the District of Columbia, the Virgin Islands, Guam, American Samoa, and the Commonwealth of the Northern Mariana Islands each have a representative called a delegate in the House. The representative of Puerto Rico is called the resident commissioner. These six people bring the concerns of their constituents to the House and have a say in some legislative proceedings. However, they may not vote on bills when the House is meeting as a whole.

FEDERAL Fact

Delegates and resident commissioners represent **territories** rather than states. Therefore, they don't have the full powers of states' representatives.

13

ONLY IN THE HOUSE

The House has special responsibilities that the Senate doesn't have. Laws about national taxes, both raising money and spending it, must begin in the House. This was the Founding Fathers' way of giving US citizens control over taxation issues.

The House must work with the Senate to accomplish some tasks. When the House considers any bill, its members usually base their votes on how the bill would affect the people of their district. If the bill passes, it goes on to the Senate for a vote. If the Senate changes the bill before passing it, the House and Senate must work together to create a bill both houses agree on. The House also decides if a government official should be impeached. The official then stands trial before the Senate, which decides if a crime has been committed and if the official should be removed from office.

FEDERAL *Fact*

Two presidents were impeached by the House but later **acquitted** by the Senate: Andrew Johnson and William Clinton.

Impeachment of Richard Nixon

In July 1974, the House Judiciary Committee voted to impeach President Richard Nixon. The three reasons for impeachment included **obstruction** of justice, abuse of power, and **contempt** of Congress. The case revolved around a break-in at the Democratic National Committee headquarters in the Watergate office building. Nixon—a Republican in his second presidential term—admitted on tape to covering up his involvement. Before the full House could vote on the impeachment, Nixon resigned the presidency.

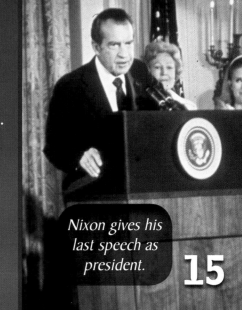

Nixon gives his last speech as president.

15

SPEAKERS, LEADERS, AND WHIPS

With 435 members, the House of Representatives needs a lot of organization in order to get things done. Certain leadership roles help smooth the legislative process. The leader of the House is called the Speaker. The Speaker is elected by the House members and serves a 2-year term. This position is required by the US Constitution and is considered the most powerful position in the House.

Besides performing the normal duties of a representative, the Speaker determines when bills will be **debated** and voted on. The Speaker also leads, or chairs, their party's steering committee, which decides which members belong to each committee. Because of this busy schedule, the Speaker rarely chairs regular meetings of the House. However, the Speaker chairs special joint sessions of Congress.

FEDERAL Fact

Nancy Pelosi of California was the first woman elected Speaker of the House.

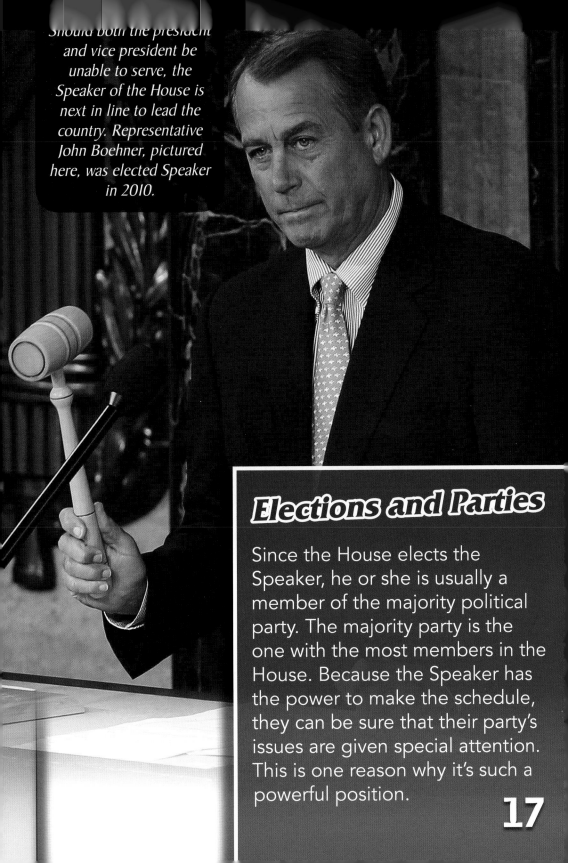

Should both the president and vice president be unable to serve, the Speaker of the House is next in line to lead the country. Representative John Boehner, pictured here, was elected Speaker in 2010.

Elections and Parties

Since the House elects the Speaker, he or she is usually a member of the majority political party. The majority party is the one with the most members in the House. Because the Speaker has the power to make the schedule, they can be sure that their party's issues are given special attention. This is one reason why it's such a powerful position.

17

There are other leaders within the House besides the Speaker. The majority and minority leaders are the spokespeople for the two political parties in the House. While the majority leader goes by the title "majority leader," the minority leader is usually called the Republican or Democratic leader, depending on which party has fewer members in the House. Both speak on behalf of their party, and they communicate with each other regarding disagreements.

The majority whip is elected by the majority party to round up support for legislation important to their party. The minority whip does the same for their party, making sure the party is united in support of or opposition to a bill. Rather than being called the minority whip, this representative is called the Republican or Democratic whip.

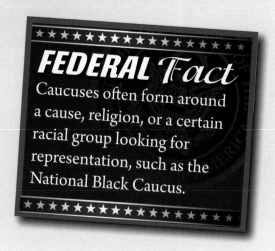

FEDERAL *Fact*

Caucuses often form around a cause, religion, or a certain racial group looking for representation, such as the National Black Caucus.

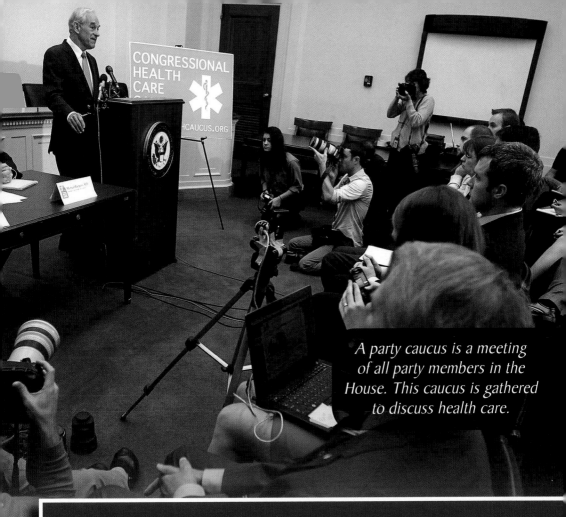

A party caucus is a meeting of all party members in the House. This caucus is gathered to discuss health care.

Caucuses

The term "caucus" comes from an Algonquin Indian word meaning "gathering of tribal chiefs." Congressional caucuses gather to discuss issues. Party leadership is also elected in party caucuses. During each legislative session, a caucus must register as a Congressional Member Organization through the House of Representatives by giving its name and purpose, along with a list of caucus officers. The caucus discussion may decide if an issue will lead to a bill.

COMMITTEES AT WORK

As many as 2,000 bills come before the House each year. Small groups called committees consider bills before they're brought before the full House. President Woodrow Wilson once wrote: "Congress in its committee rooms is Congress at work." He meant that the hardest legislative work is done in congressional committees.

The House has 20 permanent, or standing, committees. These committees are permanent because they focus on issues of continuing concern, such as education, agriculture, and foreign affairs. Party leaders decide each committee's size. The number of members from each party is based on the **ratio** of majority to minority members in the full House.

In addition to considering bills, committees have other responsibilities. Each committee watches over agencies and programs that deal with the issues on which it focuses.

Subcommittees

Most congressional committees have subcommittees. These are even smaller groups that focus on specific issues and report back to the larger committee. For example, the House Committee for Energy and Commerce has subcommittees on health; the environment and the economy; and commerce, manufacturing, and trade. Most committees and subcommittees have Internet websites with the names of their members and details about the work they do.

FEDERAL *Fact*

Select committees investigate matters that don't fit within the realm of the standing committees.

Central Intelligence Agency Director David Petraeus speaks to the House Select Intelligence Committee and Senate Intelligence Committee during a joint hearing on September 13, 2011.

Director Petraeus

On the legislative schedule, there are many entries for "hearings" and "markups." Committees and subcommittees hold hearings to gather information before making decisions about legislation. Experts on the issue may be asked to speak. Sometimes famous people, such as movie stars or athletes, are invited in order to bring more attention to a matter. Private citizens may also request to speak on the subject. Hearings are usually open to the public.

After the hearings, the committees and subcommittees may hold a markup. That is, they may suggest changes to a bill based on the new information. Markups are open to the public as well. If a committee chooses to "table" a bill, or delay work on it, it's likely to never come to a vote in the whole House.

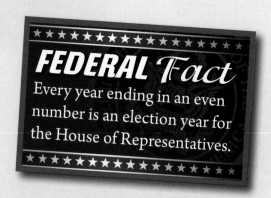

FEDERAL *Fact*
Every year ending in an even number is an election year for the House of Representatives.

A group of representatives and senators attend a hearing about the economy in September 2011.

Earmarks and Pork Barrels

Earmarks and pork barrel spending are often issues in the news. These are smaller items attached to bills or the federal budget. Earmarks are funds for certain states' and communities' needs, such as a history museum or park. They're a way for a representative to help their district. Pork barrels are rewards for businesses or groups that have helped a representative get elected. If the bill or budget passes, so do the earmarks and pork barrel items attached to it.

LET'S LEGISLATE!

How does a law get made in the House? First, at least one representative must decide to support, or sponsor, a bill. The bill then goes to committees and subcommittees to be studied and changed. When it's approved there, it moves to the whole House of Representatives.

The bill is debated, and then goes to a vote. A quorum—or minimum number of representatives—must be present for a vote. Currently, the quorum is 218 members, and usually only a majority is needed for passage. A vote to "recommit" the bill means it goes back to the committee for changes. If the bill is passed, it goes to the Senate. There it goes through a similar process. Once the House and Senate approve the bill in the same form, it goes to the president.

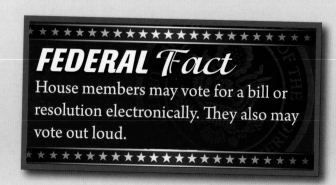

FEDERAL Fact

House members may vote for a bill or resolution electronically. They also may vote out loud.

Resolutions

A joint resolution is similar to a bill in that it usually needs approval by the House, Senate, and president before becoming law. However, joint resolutions may go on to states—not the president—for approval if they're to become constitutional amendments. Concurrent resolutions need approval from the House and Senate. These are usually rules, not laws, that have to do with Congress. Simple resolutions are only voted on in the House and only affect how the House runs.

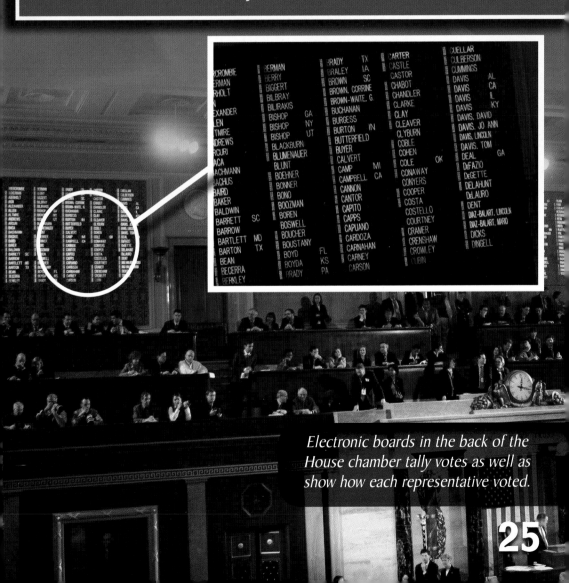

Electronic boards in the back of the House chamber tally votes as well as show how each representative voted.

BEHIND THE SCENES

There are some people who serve the House behind the scenes. The clerk checks attendance on the first day of Congress. He or she receives messages from the president and Senate when the House is not in session. He or she keeps a record of what happens in the House each day in the special House journal. The clerk also takes care of all official documents and records in the House.

The sergeant at arms is the House law enforcement chief. Safety and order are the sergeant's concern—for representatives and any visitors. The sergeant also has a **mace** to warn arguing members to calm down!

The chief administrative officer is one of the newest positions in the House, begun in 1995. This official helps with the day-to-day management of payroll, bills, and parking among other duties.

FEDERAL *Fact*

Nineteen presidents and 33 presidential candidates have served in the House of Representatives, including George H. W. Bush, Al Gore, Richard Nixon, and John F. Kennedy.

Lobbyists

Lobbyists are people paid to persuade members of Congress to support or oppose pieces of legislation. They work for businesses and organizations. Lobbyists often have a negative image, but the constitutional rights to free speech and petition protect them. While lobbyists are allowed to present information to Congress, it's illegal for them to buy a congressmember's vote with money or by other means. Sometimes former members of Congress become lobbyists after they leave office.

TALK TO YOUR REPS!

Any US citizen—including you—can contact their representative. After all, your representative is representing you, your family, and your community. If there's an issue you think they should know about, you can make an appointment to meet with them in your congressional district or in Washington, DC. You can also send an e-mail or write a letter.

If you want to know your representative's legislative schedule, you can find it online at the House's official website. You may be able to watch video of the legislative process at work, too. The more you learn about the issues facing our nation, the better you can decide who can best represent you in the House. And perhaps you can represent your congressional district yourself someday.

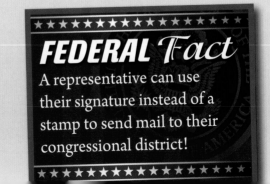

FEDERAL *Fact*

A representative can use their signature instead of a stamp to send mail to their congressional district!

How Many Seats in the House Does Your State Have?

California	53 seats	Kentucky	6 seats
Texas	32 seats	Iowa	5 seats
New York	29 seats	Oklahoma	5 seats
Florida	25 seats	Oregon	5 seats
Illinois	19 seats	Connecticut	5 seats
Pennsylvania	19 seats	Mississippi	4 seats
Ohio	18 seats	Arkansas	4 seats
Michigan	15 seats	Kansas	4 seats
New Jersey	13 seats	Nevada	3 seats
North Carolina	13 seats	Nebraska	3 seats
Georgia	13 seats	New Mexico	3 seats
Virginia	10 seats	Utah	3 seats
Massachusetts	10 seats	West Virginia	3 seats
Tennessee	9 seats	New Hampshire	2 seats
Missouri	9 seats	Idaho	2 seats
Washington	9 seats	Maine	2 seats
Indiana	9 seats	Rhode Island	2 seats
Wisconsin	8 seats	Hawaii	2 seats
Arizona	8 seats	North Dakota	1 seat
Minnesota	8 seats	Vermont	1 seat
Maryland	8 seats	Montana	1 seat
Louisiana	7 seats	Delaware	1 seat
Alabama	7 seats	South Dakota	1 seat
Colorado	7 seats	Alaska	1 seat
South Carolina	6 seats	Wyoming	1 seat

acquit: to officially declare that somebody is not guilty

census: an official count of a population

constituent: a person who lives in a congressional district

constitution: a written statement outlining the basic laws by which a country is governed

contempt: the crime of disobeying or disrespecting an authority such as a court or legislative body

debate: to discuss an issue by presenting all sides

impeach: to charge a government official with wrongdoing while in office

mace: a rod with a decorative head carried by an official as a symbol of authority

obstruction: the act of blocking or delaying business

petition: an appeal or request to a higher authority

ratio: a relationship between two different numbers

reapportion: to divide and assign something again among different groups

territory: a part of the United States that isn't within any state and has its own legislature

FOR MORE INFORMATION

Books

Dubois, Muriel L. *The U.S. House of Representatives*. Mankato, MN: Capstone Press, 2004.

Fein, Eric. *The U.S. Congress*. Mankato, MN: Capstone Press, 2008.

Koestler-Grack, Rachel A. *The House of Representatives*. New York, NY: Chelsea House, 2007.

Websites

The House of Representatives
bensguide.gpo.gov/3-5/government/national/house.html
Read more about the House, Congress, and other branches of the US government.

United States House of Representatives
www.house.gov
Check out the official site for the US House of Representatives.

INDEX